C000129591

In an Australian Light

In an Australian Light

Photographs from
across the country

Thames & Hudson

CO N
CO T S

Rural
8—47

Urban
48—81

Introduction
7

TEN

Coast
82—117

Outback
118—151

Contributors
152—153

Image Credits
154—158

Acknowledgements
159

Left to right: Great Otway National Park, Victoria;
Victoria; New South Wales; Maroochydore, Queensland

Introduction

Australia is always vivid. Here, the sun's light illuminates jewel-toned oceans, rich red soil, warm-hued sand and rocks, and the deep-green leaves of gum trees, whose trunks look like they have been painted with an Impressionist's brush. These trees reach up to a beautiful deep-blue sky that is often spotted with brilliant white clouds. In the tropical north, rainforests provide dense canopies where the harsh rays are filtered into a soft yellow. This continent's rich natural history has created a unique landscape that glows with the sun's brilliance.

People experience natural light differently depending on where they live, though the source is the same: the massive sphere of plasma that is our sun. Out in the cold void of space are giant gas clouds filled with the ingredients to make stars; the low temperature causes atoms in the gas to bind together to form heavier molecules, and their gravity pulls surrounding material to them. With growing mass and fixed space, the density rapidly increases, forming enormous clumps that fragment away from the larger cloud.

About five billion years ago, one of these clumps grew so large that it became unstable. Collapsing under its own gravity, it transformed into a spinning disk surrounding a massive core. Material continued to fall onto the core, driving the heat up. Finally, the pressure became too great; in the centre of the core, hydrogen atoms were smashed together, igniting a nuclear furnace that we know as the sun. Since then, the sun has been fusing hundreds of tons of hydrogen into helium per second. The process releases incredible amounts of energy – energy that we see as light.

Earth is a spinning sphere that travels around the sun. The shape of our planet allows it to receive more direct sunlight where it bulges outward, at the equator. Here, life thrives and the sun's rays reflect on tropical landscapes, revealing rich and vibrant colours. As you travel north or south of the equator, the light is angled, diminishing its intensity. The solar rays that reach the poles are even weaker, allowing frigid conditions to persist. The absence of flora and the presence of snow and ice create a bright environment dominated by cool colours.

But the sun does not shine all the time. Once every 24 hours, the Earth rotates. Over this interval, parts of the world are bathed in the sun's light, while others are denied it. Without sunlight, our world changes, but it is not completely devoid of light. In fact, for some this is the best time to collect light from distant stars and galaxies or to capture moonlit vistas.

Unless you live near the equator, the amount of sunlight you receive changes throughout the year. Seasons exist because billions of years ago, the Earth was hit by another forming planet close in size to Mars, and the force of the impact tilted the Earth. As our planet makes its yearly journey around the sun, parts of its surface receive changing amounts of direct light, which alters the length of our days and nights and drives weather patterns.

From December to early March, the southern hemisphere is tilted towards the sun, and Australia enters summer. The sun's rays bake the red centre, wind dries out the south-east, and coastal cities become more humid. From late May through August, the southern hemisphere is tilted away from the sun and on average receives less direct light, leading to shorter days and cooler temperatures. In the intervening months, we experience spring and autumn, transition times when the hemispheres receive equal portions of the sun's light.

The shape of our planet allows it to receive more direct sunlight where it bulges outward, at the equator. Here, life thrives and the sun's rays reflect on tropical landscapes, revealing rich and vibrant colours. As you travel north or south of the equator, the light is angled, diminishing its intensity.

The seasons govern how our landscapes are illuminated. More light brings more colours, but the accompanying heat can turn vibrant green vistas into rich earth-coloured scenes. With grey clouds and less direct light, our world displays a palette of muted colours.

There is much beauty to be found in our atmosphere, the complex mixture of molecules and particles that plays an important role in absorbing high-energy UV radiation. Moisture in the atmosphere bends the light that shines through it; this is why stars near the horizon twinkle and why astronomers try to find the driest places on Earth to get a crisp view of the heavens. High concentrations of moisture and particles in the air create more ways for light to be reflected and bent, and so we are treated to the spectacle of sunsets as the sun moves close to the horizon and its light must travel through more air. The sunsets seen from coastal areas to sheep paddocks around Australia are some of the most colourful in the world. Meanwhile, the relatively low pollution levels of the southern hemisphere mean that more of the sun's light reaches us.

Light affects us deeply as human beings. We would not exist without it, and it continues to play an important role in our biological processes. Even UV radiation, which can be harmful in large amounts, helps our absorption of essential vitamins at a young age. Our sleep cycle that allows us to rest and restore is intertwined with light. Yet in our urge to create safe places, we are also concealing starscapes: children born in large cities go too long without experiencing the vast wonder of a night sky. We must go further and further away from cities and towns to enjoy this extraordinary natural phenomenon.

Light is not just a necessity; it is one of our most important tools. We have learned how to count it, bend it, create it and shape it. Classically, we have used light to extinguish the darkness. Now, we use light to create art, to capture landscapes and distant galaxies.

Dr Rebecca Allen

RU
R
RU
AL

Opening page: Minjah, Victoria
Previous page: Katoomba, New South Wales
Above and right: Castlemaine, Victoria

Above: Boggabri, New South Wales
Right: Tocal, New South Wales

Katoomba, New South Wales

Left and above: High Country, Victoria

Above: Avon Valley, Western Australia
Right: Deniliquin, New South Wales

Above and right: Near Lake Boga, Victoria

Above: Blackall, Queensland
Right: Byron Bay, New South Wales
Following page: Duranillin, Western Australia

Left to right: Glenlusk, Tasmania; Dampier, Western Australia;
Wombat, New South Wales; Wombat, New South Wales

Above: Eugenana, Tasmania
Right: Quirindi, New South Wales
Following page: Darwin, Northern Territory

Left to right: Avon Valley, Western Australia; Queenscliff, Victoria;
Broome, Western Australia

Above: Young, New South Wales
Right: Near Young, New South Wales

Left: Victoria
Above: Pine Grove, Victoria

Above: Near Hawks Nest, New South Wales
Right: Mount Solitary, New South Wales

Left: Lockyer National Park, Queensland
Above, left to right: Bremer Bay, Western Australia;
Singleton, New South Wales

Left to right: Yambuk, Victoria; Blackall, Queensland;
Singleton, New South Wales; Victoria
Following page: Grampians National Park, Victoria

UR

BAN

Opening page: Melbourne, Victoria
Left: Young, New South Wales
Above: Inverell, New South Wales

Above and right: Melbourne, Victoria

Fitzroy, Victoria

Above: Near Little River, Victoria
Right: Antwerp, Victoria

32 BATTALION
33 BATTALION
34 BATTALION
35 BATTALION
36 BATTALION
27 BATTALION
40 BATTALION
41 BATTALION
42 BATTALION
43 BATTALION
44 BATTALION
45 BATTALION
46 BATTALION
47 BATTALION
51 BATTALION
52 BATTALION
53 BATTALION
54 BATTALION
55 BATTALION
55/53 BATTALION
58/59 BATTALION
61 BATTALION

BURRELL
BYRN...
CARR
CARTER
COOK E. H
CRACKNELL
CURTIS R.G.
...TIS S.G.
...VIS A.L.C.
...AY J.W.
...NNIS W.E.R.
...NSLEY G.R.
EDDY C.McW.
EVANS L.C.
...VERINGHAM W.L.
...AGAN W.J.
...OOD W.E.
...ANKS A.B.
...ASER R.A.
...EORGE A.J.
...EYER K.V.
...HIGGIOLI E.K.
...LASSON R.C.
GODFREY T.J.
...LLIFORD H.A.
...NAY J.D.
...RMAN R.A.
...RRISON R.
...RVEY C.R.
...LLMAN R.E.
...NRY J.K.
...NSON C.F.
...GHLAND C.
...BS H.
HOGAN A.J.
HOOK W.
HOPKINS F.E.
...OTTES E.S.
...UGHES F.R.
HYATT J.R.
IRVINE F.A.
JACKSON C.
...RRETT J.L.
...LY B.G.
...AIRD D.A.
...AMBERT L.A.
...AMBLE G.R.
...AMBORN W.G.
...AMONT W.
...EES R.
...ITTLE D.
...OWE W.J.
...OWTHER C.B.
...ONS M.S.
McALIECE C.G.
...cDIARMID A.
...acDOUGALL D.

PIC...
POLL...
POTTER...
RAE F...
RAMSAY
REED G.B.
REEVES S.J.
RIEDELL L.G.
ROBERTS R.S.
ROBERTS S.L.
SADLER F.H.
SAMPSON K.J.
SAUER C.A.
SCHIFFMANN H.F.
SEARCY M.R.
SEATER L.L.
SHAW T.A.
SHERWIN H.V.
SIBRAA L.S.
SLAVEN B.J.
SMITH E.D.
SMITH F.W.
SMITH H.P.
SMITH R.B.
SQUIRE I.B.
STANTON E.C.
STARKEY A.G.
STEWART L.W.
TAYLOR W.E.
THOMPSON W.H.
THOMSON J.A.
THORNTON I.
TIPPETTS W.A.
TOLE & F.M.
TURNER D.G.
TURNER D.J.
TURNER O.G.
TURNER W.S.J.
UHLMAN S.G.
WALKER W.A.
WATSON T.B.
WILLDING L.R.
WOODWARD C.J.
WOOLLEY F.S.
YERBURY R.H.

No. 2 INDEPENDENT COMPANY

...IREY D.H.
...LEXANDER R.G.
...ORD F.
...ALMERS R.S.&
...HISWELL T.A.
...OTSWORTH H.B.
...ROWDER R.
...AN E.
...ANNON B.
...OGG K.
...KNIGHT P.
...ANE A.
...ARRIOTT H.W.
...ITCHELL H.E.
...ULQUEENEY G.

MURRAY R.H.
OLIVER R.
PEARCE R.E.
POLLARD I.
RICHARDS K.J.
SIMPSON I.P.
SMEATON A.
SMITH F.G.
STANTON G.
SWIFT R.R.
THOMAS G.E.
WALKER J.W.
WALLER
YEATES A.

.../3 INDEPENDENT COMPANY

...UCKLE R.
...KKA J.
LAMB B.A.
LATIMER T.M.

No. 4 INDEPENDENT COMPANY

...L S.W.
...NAN W.J.
...TNESS D.H.
...URIGAN E.
...WELL E.G.
...LIOS G.
...UGTON G.A.
MASON N.
O DEA O.D.
PURSS V.J.
WILLIAMS O.R.

.../5 & 5 INDEPENDENT COMPANIES

...EZARD J.W.W.
...ONNELL J.M.
...OOTH R.D.
...RUFORD A.P.R.
...ULLOCK W.W.
...REEK D.L.
...ELLIN A.H.
...SDALE W.
HAMES N.W.
HOBBS L.E.R.
KNEEN T.P.
LEITCH J.C.
McCALLUM M.J.
PEDDER E.A.
SMITH D.N.K.
WILSON T.G.

.../6 & 6 INDEPENDENT COMPANIES

...AVEN I.A.J.
...AND O.W.
HALL E.W.
SANDOR L.

.../7 INDEPENDENT COMPANY

...OWN W.A.

BBO...
DOL...
DRED...
LLCHIN...
LLEN...
ALLEN K.
NGUS...
MSTRO...
SHFORD...
KINSON...
TWOOD...
AILEY...
AKER...
ANFIELD...
...
BATTEN...
BEADLE...
BEAUMO...
BELL A.
BENNETT...
BIESSE...
BILLING...
LAKE A...
BLOSSETT...
BOCK E...
OND...
OREHAM...
OSCHER...
OULD...
OURNE...
...

...WY
...A.I.
...R.J.
BENDALL B.
BENNETT H.
BIGGS G.
...C.R.
...OP H.
...CKBORR...
...OTH H.
...ORROW L.
...AZIER A.
...RENNAN
...GGS
...OOKER
...BROWN A.
...BROWN R.
...OWN R.
...OWN S.
...ROWNE M.
...ROWNING
...UCKLEY
...GG F.
...OCK
...RKE J.
...HELL
...AS C.
...TON E.
...TCHER
...LER T.
...ERON
...NNON
...RLILE
...R.I.
...RRUTHE...
...ARTER A.
...ARTER
...ASE W.C.
...HAMB...
...HAPMAN
...WERS

...NE GUN BATTALION

HEDGER W.R.
HENDERSON J.M.
HILL D.W.
HILL J.E.
HOBBY E.R.
HOFFMANN
HOLLAND
HOOPER R.
HORE S.
JAMES A.
JARVIS
...RRIS
JENKINS
JENKIN
JENKINS
JENNINGS
JOHNSON
JONAS
JONES
JOSH...
KERIN
KIMPTON
LINDGREN
...OTT A.
...ADMAN
...ANGLEY
...ECKIE
...ETTE
...ILFORD E.G.
...INS
...RE A.
...OCKWOOD
LUCAS R.
LYNN
...DONALD
McGEORGE W.
McGINNIS M.
...REGOR I.D.
...NTOSH
McKENZIE A.
McLEAN P.N.
MESHIMMINE
...ARCHANT
...ARTIN
...MAY
MILLER E.H.J.
MILLS D.F.
...NDUE R.N.
MITCHELL F.J.
MOREY A.E.
McUNSEY J.
MOYES
MULLER

Previous page: Canberra, Australian Capital Territory
Above: Melbourne, Victoria
Right: Brisbane, Queensland

Left: Dromana, Victoria
Above: Brisbane, Queensland

Above, left to right: Young, New South Wales; Port Macquarie, New South Wales
Right: Young, New South Wales

Left to right: Collingwood, Victoria; Melbourne, Victoria; Launceston, Tasmania;
Queenscliff, Victoria

Harden, New South Wales

Above: Millers Point, New South Wales
Right: Fremantle, Western Australia
Following page: Beechworth, Victoria

Left to right: Port Fairy, Victoria; Victoria; Atherton Tableland, Queensland

Left to right: Lurg, Victoria; Sydney, New South Wales;
Freshwater Beach, New South Wales; Sydney, New South Wales

Above: Sydney, New South Wales
Right: Kirribilli, New South Wales
Following page: Pyrmont, New South Wales

COAST

Opening page: Torquay, Victoria
Previous page: Bondi, New South Wales
Above, left to right: Victoria; North Stradbroke Island, Queensland;
Albany, Western Australia; Rainbow Beach, Queensland

Above: Bondi Beach, New South Wales
Right: Glenelg, South Australia
Following page: North Bondi, New South Wales

Above and right: Maroochydore, Queensland

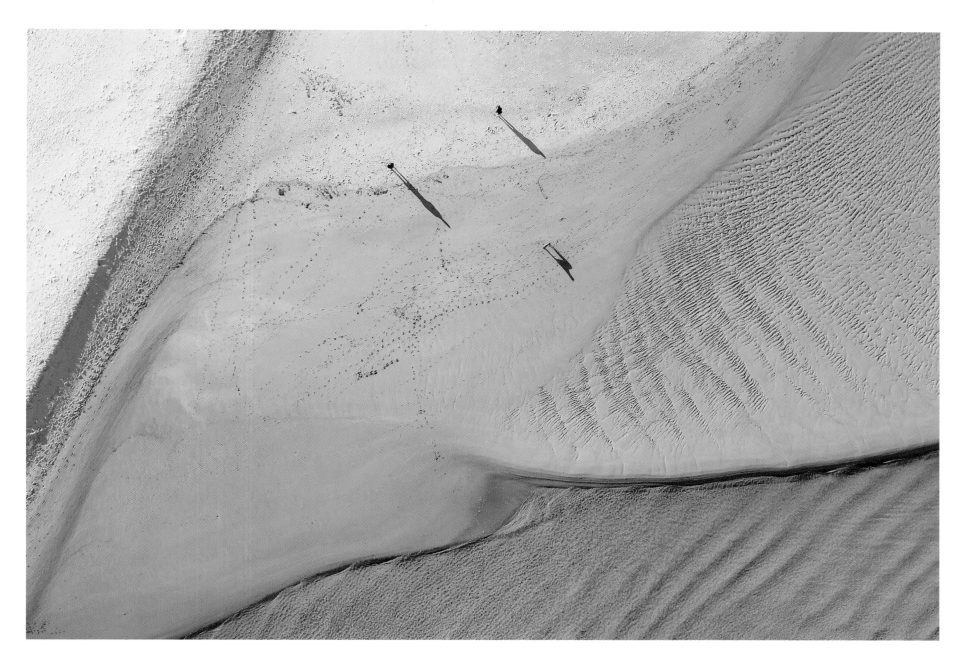

Myponga, South Australia

Above: South Alligator, Northern Territory
Right: Mount Martha, Victoria

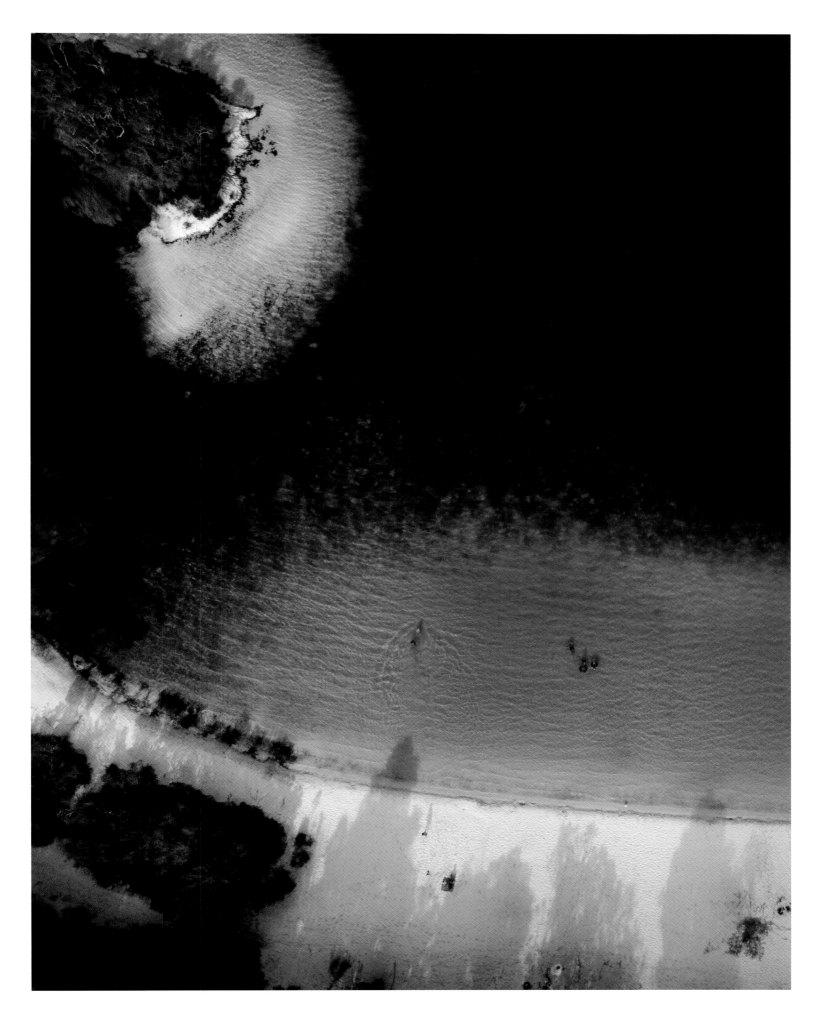

Previous page: Princetown, Victoria
Left: Hyams Beach, New South Wales
Above: Fraser Island, Queensland

Stradbroke Island, Queensland

Left: Port Macquarie, New South Wales
Above: Willunga, South Australia
Following page: Lennox Heads, New South Wales

Above: Melbourne, Victoria
Right: Brighton, Victoria

Left to right: Darwin, Northern Territory; Beachmere, Queensland;
Flinders, Victoria; Forestier Peninsula, Tasmania

Darwin, Northern Territory

Above: Eyre Peninsula, South Australia
Right: Bells Beach, Victoria

Above: Bradleys Head, New South Wales
Right: Wollongong, New South Wales

Opening page: Olary, South Australia
Previous page: Gemtree, Northern Territory
Above, left to right: Eidsvold, Queensland; Warooka, South Australia;
Port Fairy, Victoria; Near Kakadu, Northern Territory

Previous page: Arnhem Land, Northern Territory
Above: Kakadu National Park, Northern Territory

Above: Thargomindah, Queensland
Right: Kanku-Breakaways Conservation Park, South Australia

Above: Burra, South Australia
Right: Thargomindah, Queensland

Previous page: Coniston Station, Northern Territory
Above: Karlu Karlu / Devils Marbles Conservation Reserve, Northern Territory
Right: Blackall, Queensland

Nitmiluk National Park, Northern Territory

Left: Litchfield National Park, Northern Territory
Above: Roebuck Bay, Western Australia

Left to right: Coalseam Conservation Park, Western Australia;
Near William Creek, South Australia; Wombat, New South Wales;
Wombeyan Caves, New South Wales

Nitmiluk National Park, Northern Territory

Left: Mungo, New South Wales
Above: Near Mirannie, Hunter Valley, New South Wales

Above: Wycliffe Well, Northern Territory
Right: Silverton, New South Wales

Above: Howard Springs, Northern Territory
Following page: Flinders Ranges, South Australia

Contributors

DR REBECCA ALLEN
Dr Rebecca Allen completed her PhD in astrophysics at Swinburne University of Technology in Melbourne, VIC. Her research focuses on understanding the evolution and growth of galaxies over time, going all the way back to when the universe was barely a billion years old. Now part of Swinburne's Space Office and the manager of Swinburne Astronomy Productions, she uses her scientific expertise and enthusiasm to communicate the wonders of the universe to others and to create inspiring and transformative learning experiences. When she moved from the United States to Australia in 2012, two things grabbed Dr Allen's attention: the moon was upside down and the sky was the deepest blue she had ever seen. Since that day, she has come to realise that the Australian light is special. It reveals a rich and vibrant palette of colours like nowhere else in the world.

LISA ALEXANDER
Lisa Alexander lives in outback QLD, 90 kilometres from the closest town. She loves to capture moments of beauty in everyday life and has always been fascinated by photography and the documenting of never-to-be-repeated moments and emotions.
www.lisaalexanderphotography.com.au

DANIELLE BEIERMANN
Danielle Beiermann loves capturing the simple things, the sun beaming through trees, fluffy clouds and wildlife. Every now and then she photographs the amazing night sky, and brings it to life.

MELISSA BERNARD
Melissa Bernard grew up on a small farm and had the ultimate childhood: fresh country air, surrounded by animals, beautiful countryside and an assortment of old farmers full of life and stories. She loves meeting people and being able to capture their stories in the form of photographs.
www.melissabernardphotography.com

CHARLIE BLACKER
Charlie Blacker is a passionate landscape, nature and adventure photographer. He lives and works out of a self-built camper van, travelling and exploring Australia. If he doesn't have a camera in his hand, you'll find him in the surf or fixing his van.

CHLOE DE BRITO
Chloe de Brito is a filmmaker and photographer from Sydney, NSW. She's interested in light and shadows in both urban and natural environments.
www.chloe-debrito.com

GARY CHAPMAN
Gary Chapman was hooked on photography at the age of 14, when he learned to use an old Kodak 126. He made a drastic career change, as his interest in his hobby rapidly overtook his career aspirations. For Gary, there is no greater thrill than watching the light change and transform a landscape.
www.photographers.com.au/garychapman

TERRY COOKE
Terry Cooke's main focus over the last few years has been recording the many and varied landscapes and urban environments of the Northern Tablelands of NSW. Terry has both exhibited and produced books of photography and also enjoys photographing local drama and musical productions, capturing images while travelling around Australia and teaching photography.

CRAIG CROSTHWAITE
After 30 years working his dream job in the advertising industry, Craig Crosthwaite embarked on a new adventure and studied photography; he hasn't put the camera down since. Photography allows him to combine a love of the ocean with newly acquired skills.

LOUISE DENTON
Primarily a landscape and nature photographer in the Top End of Australia, Louise Denton is based in Darwin, NT. She travels around the iconic areas of Kakadu, Litchfield and Katherine.
www.louisedenton.com

CHERI DESAILLY
Cheri Desailly combines her passion for photography with a love of the environment and wildlife.
www.cheridesailly.com

ROSALIE DIBBEN
Living in a rural area and travelling into pastoral and semi-remote areas allows Rosalie Dibben to see some of the less common parts of this amazing country. Picking up a camera always helps her relax, and she loves capturing the moments and sights that catch her eye anywhere she goes.

CARLA DIBBS
Sunsets spent with loved ones, the rush of the ocean, and a coffee with the soundtrack of rain are the moments that form the essence of Carla Dibbs's photography.

MIKE DISBURY
Mike Disbury enjoys bushwalking to parts of WA that you can't drive to, and recording beautiful images.

KERRY DUNLOP
Kerry Dunlop is an amateur photographer based in sunny QLD. She takes her camera with her everywhere because she never wants to miss a shot.
www.kaddunphoto.com

CLARE FARRELLY
Clare Farrelly is a young Australian photographer with a passion for capturing special memories and moments in time. Her love of photography began with capturing small details: things she found in the shed, yard, in her town – things close to her heart.
www.clearlightphotography.com.au

NAOMI FENTON
Naomi Fenton is a secondary school teacher and photographer based in Burnie on the north-western coast of TAS. She loves capturing the small details of this beautiful part of the world and its people.
www.lookseebynaomifenton.com

LACHLAN GARDINER
Lachlan Gardiner's driving passion in life is to see and experience new places, meet new people and live a life full of adventure. As a photographer, Lachlan enjoys spending time in the outdoors and capturing the amazing landscapes that exist in this world, particularly the vast and diverse topography of Australia.
www.lachlangardiner.com

ELISE GARNER
Elise Garner is a photographer, coffee addict and beach lover. Delicious, warm or soft light is her weakness and her strength.
www.lecoco.com.au

MICHAEL HALL
Michael Hall's work focuses on exploring human impact on the environment, including the causes and effects of climate change, to improve ecological awareness.
www.michaelhall.net

FOREST HARDER
Forest Harder is a photographer from SA who's mostly self-taught. He has travelled to many parts of the globe as well as throughout Australia. Forest spends a lot of time in the outdoors, exploring, hiking and photographing. He loves the connection to nature that photography gives him.
www.forestharderimages.com.au

DAVID HICKS
David Hicks has been a professional musician for over 25 years, 16 of those serving full-time as a member of the Australian Army Band Corps. His interest in photography started in high school as a hobby, but over the years the passion has grown. He still gets excited every time he picks up the camera, knowing that as a photographer he is recording his own part of history.
www.davehicksphotography.com

CRAIG HOLLOWAY
After working as a commercial photographer in Ballarat, VIC, for eight years, Craig Holloway and his partner, Paula, decided to travel around the country. Craig's 'Abandoned Places' photographs document the forgotten and forlorn.
www.craighollowayphotographer.com

JODIE JOHNSON
Jodie Johnson loves interiors and architecture, and capturing beautiful spaces with natural light.
www.jodiejohnson.com.au

ROBERT LANG
Robert Lang lives on a small rural sheep and cereal farm just outside of Port Lincoln, a fishing town on the tip of the Eyre Peninsula in SA. Surrounded by amazing coastline in all directions, Robert shoots anything from outback to sea and enjoys camping, hiking, bushwalking, fishing, nature, conservation, travel and documentaries.
www.robertlang.com.au

HEIDI LEWIS

Heidi Lewis loves showing the world off to the world and does this through photography, writing and teaching photography. She also loves surfing, Cuban Latin dancing, yoga and discovering new parts (or old parts over again) of the globe.

www.heidiwho.com

ANDREW MCINNES

Andrew McInnes is a photographer, sailor, cattleman, fly fisherman, naturalist, dreamer, drone pilot and sometime poet.

www.andrewmcinnes.com

JUSTIN MCKINNEY

Photography is Justin Mckinney's escape from reality.

www.500px.com/jmckinney

SCOTT MURRAY

Born in WA, Scott Murray has always been into art using various paints, pencils and pastels. He used to record images with a Kodak film camera and then transform them into paintings or drawings; now, in the digital era, he uses his artistic style to capture the world around him and share it with others.

JODIE NASH

Jodie Nash wants her photographs to lift others up. She grew up in a country town in the Mallee, VIC, but now lives on the Gold Coast, QLD. Her career as a theatre nurse means she can wake up at any hour and be ready to get out with the camera.

www.jona.com.au

ROWENA NAYLOR

Rowena Naylor is a professional stock photographer living a glorious life in country VIC. Her main portfolios cover agriculture, farming and interiors, but she also loves to capture everyday life in rural Australia.

PAUL NELSON

Paul Nelson is a professional photographer from Melbourne, VIC. He has shown his work in two successful exhibitions and has a number of his prints hanging in some of Melbourne's most famous restaurants.

www.paulnelsonphotography.com.au

MICHELLE NEWNAN

Michelle Newnan enjoys capturing her view of Australian family life.

www.michellenewnanphotography.com

JOANNE O'KEEFE

Based in Port Fairy, VIC, Joanne O'Keefe is a farmer's wife who loves creating art and food and taking photographs of all her loves. She is captivated by finding the beauty in everyday things and passionate about capturing the essence of our amazing Australia in photographs.

OLIVIA PAGE

Olivia Page documents people, cultures, nature and the human-made. Adventure, sports, travel and the outdoors – surfing, climbing, sailing, flying and highlining – dominate her work. Her photographs and words can be found in adventure, climbing, sailing and geographical magazines and journals.

www.oliviapage.com.au

SHANE PEDERSEN

Shane Pedersen grew up in QLD but has lived in TAS permanently since 2002, and has had great adventures in its many beautiful natural areas. A love of nature and spectacular wild places is what inspires Shane to go to extraordinary efforts at times to capture just the right image.

ANNE POWELL

Anne Powell lives on the coast in beautiful Port Stephens, NSW. She credits photography with having heightened her awareness of her surroundings.

NATALIE PURSLOW

Natalie Purslow specialises in natural light photography in the portrait, fashion and conceptual genres. Her journey with photography began after the tragic death of her uncle in 2001, when she inherited his Pentax and began to document the poignant aspects of her gritty neighbourhood streets and childhood in Perth, WA. Her work is moody, atmospheric and sometimes both fragile and jarring.

www.nataliepurslow.com

GARY RADLER

A husband, father, grandfather and lover of photography, Gary Radler works both as a psychologist and a photographer.

www.garyradler.com

JONAH RITCHIE

Jonah Ritchie is a Sydney, NSW-based editorial and lifestyle photographer who conceptualises ideas and produces compelling visual stories for creative agencies and marketing teams.

ANGIE ROE

A lover of light and colour, Angie Roe takes photos that speak of relaxed, natural storytelling. She has worked as a professional photographer since the days of film.

www.angieroephotography.com.au

PHOEBE ROUSE

Phoebe Rouse is a jewellery maker living on the Mornington Peninsula, VIC. Her innate love of nature, particularly the unspoiled coast of her home, inspires her creative life.

FRANCESCO SOLFRINI

Francesco Solfrini is an Italian-born and Sydney, NSW-based photographer with over five years of experience as a commercial and editorial photographer. He sees people as complex living artworks and is fascinated by ever-changing faces and personalities, who they are and what they do.

www.lefotodifrancesco.com

RUNE SVENDSEN

Rune Svendsen is a Norwegian photographer who has lived in Australia since 2013. He loves chasing interesting and unusual light conditions, and new and rare angles. Rune's base is in Sydney, NSW, but he travels interstate in Australia and annually back to Norway with his camera close at hand. His aim is to capture well-known landmarks with his very own twist.

www.svendsania.com

CARO TELFER

Caro Telfer is a rural-based, AIPP-accredited professional photographer who is married to a farmer. Her studio is in Darkan, in the wheatbelt region of WA. She loves photographing people and life in rural communities and travels to rural areas to photograph family farming operations.

www.carotelfer.com

LEAH-ANNE THOMPSON

Leah-Anne Thompson is a landscape, seascape and stock photographer from Sydney, NSW. She is drawn to beautiful places, spaces and nature.

GILLIAN VANN

Gillian Vann has travelled widely across this great big land, visiting every capital and plenty of places in between. She lived in Brisbane, QLD, for most of her life but for now calls the glorious northern beaches of Sydney, NSW, home.

www.gillianvann.com

DAVID VEENTJER

David Veentjer enjoys taking photographs of everyday life in the suburbs of Melbourne, VIC, and also overseas travel photography when lucky enough to find the time (and money!).

www.davidlukephotography.com

ASTRID VOLZKE

Working as a photojournalist for nine years has given Astrid Volzke a love of the spontaneous and unobtrusive. She lives on a property in Moodiarrup, WA, with friendly animals, a private rural campground and a huge lake.

www.astridvolzke.com

DALE WEBSTER

A need to tell stories is the driving force behind Dale Webster's photographs.

www.dalewebster.wixsite.com/photographic

JANE WORNER

An enthusiastic amateur photographer, Jane Worner started taking photos when she was an aid worker, travelling the world being inspired by people and places. The arrival of twins stopped her wanderlust lifestyle, and she started taking photos much closer to home – often in the house.

Image Credits

Contents

Joanne O'Keefe

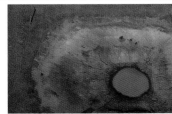
Rowena Naylor

Olivia Page

Gary Chapman

Rural

p. 8 — Joanne O'Keefe

p. 10 — Rune Svendsen

p. 12 — Gary Chapman

p. 13 — Gary Chapman

p. 14 — Clare Farrelly

p. 15 — Clare Farrelly

p. 16 — Rune Svendsen

p. 18 — Joanne O'Keefe

p. 19 — Joanne O'Keefe

p. 20 — Angie Roe

p. 21 — Chloe de Brito

p. 22 — Dale Webster

p. 23 — Dale Webster

p. 24 — Lisa Alexander

p. 25 — Carla Dibbs

p. 26 — Astrid Volzke

p. 28 — Lachlan Gardiner (left)
Caro Telfer (right)

p. 29 — Andrew McInnes (left)
Jane Worner (right)

p. 30 — Naomi Fenton

p. 31 — Clare Farrelly

p. 32 — Leah-Anne Thompson

p. 34 — Angie Roe (left)
Gary Chapman (right)

p. 35 — Justin Mckinney

p. 36 — Jane Worner

p. 37 — Joanne O'Keefe

p. 38 — Rowena Naylor

p. 39 — Dale Webster

p. 40 — Terry Cooke

p. 41 — Leah-Anne Thompson

p. 42 — Jodie Nash

p. 43 — Caro Telfer (left)
Clare Farrelly (right)

p. 44 — Lisa Alexander (left)
Joanne O'Keefe (right)

p. 45 — Rowena Naylor (left)
Clare Farrelly (right)

p. 46 — Robert Lang

Urban

p. 48 — Jodie Johnson

p. 50 — Jane Worner

p. 51 — Melissa Bernard

p. 52 — Jodie Johnson

p. 53 — Rowena Naylor

p. 54 — Phoebe Rouse

p. 56 — David Veentjer

p. 57 — Paul Nelson

p. 58 — Elise Garner

p. 60 — Jane Worner

   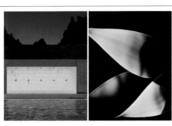 

p. 61 — Cheri Desailly

p. 62 — Phoebe Rouse

p. 63 — Gary Chapman

p. 64 — Jane Worner (left)
Charlie Blacker (right)

p. 65 — Jane Worner

p. 66 — Gary Radler (left)
Rowena Naylor (right)

p. 67 — Gary Chapman (left and right)

p. 68 — Jane Worner

p. 70 — Francesco Solfrini

p. 71 — Natalie Purslow

p. 72 — Jane Worner

p. 74 — Joanne O'Keefe (left)
Rowena Naylor (right)

p. 75 — Cheri Desailly

p. 76 — Gary Radler (left)
Anne Powell (right)

p. 77 — Michael Hall (left)
Jonah Ritchie (right)

p. 78 — Terry Cooke

p. 79 — Rune Svendsen

p. 80 — Rune Svendsen

Coast

p. 82 — Craig Holloway

p. 84 — Cheri Desailly

p. 86 — Danielle Beiermann (left)
Cheri Desailly (right)

p. 87 — Mike Disbury (left)
Andrew McInnes (right)

p. 88 — Francesco Solfrini

p. 89 — Heidi Lewis

p. 90 — Rune Svendsen

p. 92 — Gary Chapman

p. 93 — Gary Chapman

p. 94 — Forest Harder

p. 96 — Scott Murray

p. 97 — Gillian Vann

p. 98 — Rune Svendsen

p. 100 — Leah-Anne Thompson

p. 101 — Gillian Vann

p. 102 — Lachlan Gardiner

p. 104 — Charlie Blacker

p. 105 — Gillian Vann

p. 106 — Kerry Dunlop

p. 108 — Danielle Beiermann

p. 109 — Michelle Newnan

p. 110 — Louise Denton (left)
David Hicks (right)

p. 111 — Phoebe Rouse (left)
Shane Pedersen (right)

p. 112 — Louise Denton

p. 114 — Rosalie Dibben

p. 115 — Craig Crosthwaite

p. 116 — Rune Svendsen

p. 117 — Rune Svendsen

Outback

p. 118 — Andrew McInnes

p. 120 — Louise Denton

p. 122 — Andrew McInnes (left)
Rosalie Dibben (right)

p. 123 — Joanne O'Keefe (left)
Cheri Desailly (right)

p. 124 — Scott Murray

p. 126 — Louise Denton

p. 128 — Andrew McInnes

p. 129 — Craig Holloway

p. 130 — Gary Chapman

p. 131 — Andrew McInnes

p. 132 — Jonah Ritchie

p. 134 — Louise Denton

p. 135 — Lisa Alexander

p. 136 — Louise Denton

p. 138 — Louise Denton

p. 139 — Cheri Desailly

p. 140 — Rosalie Dibben (left)
Caro Telfer (right)

p. 141 — Jane Worner (left)
Leah-Anne Thompson (right)

p. 142 — Louise Denton

p. 144 — Leah-Anne Thompson

p. 145 — Clare Farrelly

p. 146 — Jodie Nash

p. 147 — Leah-Anne Thompson

p. 148 — Louise Denton

p. 150 — Rosalie Dibben

Acknowledgements

Many thanks to the photographers who responded from across the country to our call for images of the Australian landscape in all its guises and every light. A special thanks to Claire Bonnor, Director, Austockphoto for all of her help and advice and for making an unwieldy process drama free.

First published in Australia in 2019
by Thames & Hudson Australia Pty Ltd
11 Central Boulevard, Portside Business Park
Port Melbourne, Victoria 3207
ABN: 72 004 751 964

www.thamesandhudson.com.au

22 21 20 19   5 4 3 2 1

The moral right of the author has been asserted.

Thames & Hudson Australia wishes to acknowledge that
Aboriginal and Torres Strait Islander people are the first
storytellers of this nation and the traditional custodians of the
land on which we live and work. We acknowledge their continuing
culture and pay respect to Elders past, present and future.

978 1 7607604 7 2

A catalogue record for this
book is available from the
National Library of Australia

Front cover: Jonah Ritchie, *Lone ghost gum tree and spinifex
grass*, Coniston Station, north of Alice Springs, Northern Territory
Back cover: Heidi Lewis, *People on the sand and in the water
at the beach*, Glenelg, South Australia
Design: Claire Orrell
Editing: Jo Turner
Printed and bound in China by 1010